Dear Parents:

Congratulations! Your child is taking the first steps on an exciting journey. The destination? Independent reading!

STEP INTO READING® will help your child get there. The program offers five steps to reading success. Each step includes fun stories and colorful art or photographs. In addition to original fiction and books with favorite characters, there are Step into Reading Non-Fiction Readers, Phonics Readers and Boxed Sets, Sticker Readers, and Comic Readers—a complete literacy program with something to interest every child.

Learning to Read, Step by Step!

Ready to Read   Preschool–Kindergarten
• big type and easy words • rhyme and rhythm • picture clues
For children who know the alphabet and are eager to begin reading.

Reading with Help   Preschool–Grade 1
• basic vocabulary • short sentences • simple stories
For children who recognize familiar words and sound out new words with help.

Reading on Your Own   Grades 1–3
• engaging characters • easy-to-follow plots • popular topics
For children who are ready to read on their own.

Reading Paragraphs   Grades 2–3
• challenging vocabulary • short paragraphs • exciting stories
For newly independent readers who read simple sentences with confidence.

Ready for Chapters   Grades 2–4
• chapters • longer paragraphs • full-color art
For children who want to take the plunge into chapter books but still like colorful pictures.

STEP INTO READING® is designed to give every child a successful reading experience. The grade levels are only guides; children will progress through the steps at their own speed, developing confidence in their reading. The F&P Text Level on the back cover serves as another tool to help you choose the right book for your child.

Remember, a lifetime love of reading starts with a single step!

Text copyright © 1987 by Penguin Random House LLC
Cover art and interior illustrations copyright © 1987 by Freire Wright

All rights reserved. Published in the United States by Random House Children's Books, a division of Penguin Random House LLC, New York.

Step into Reading, Random House, and the Random House colophon are registered trademarks of Penguin Random House LLC.

Visit us on the Web!
StepIntoReading.com
rhcbooks.com

Educators and librarians, for a variety of teaching tools, visit us at RHTeachersLibrarians.com

Library of Congress Cataloging-in-Publication Data is available upon request.
ISBN 978-0-394-88716-6 (trade) — ISBN 978-1-5247-6601-6 (ebook)

Printed in the United States of America
50 49 48 47 46 45 44 43 42 41

This book has been officially leveled by using the F&P Text Level Gradient™ Leveling System.

Noah's Ark
A Story from the Bible

by Linda Hayward
illustrated by Freire Wright

Random House 🏠 New York

Noah lived long ago.

He was a good man.

He listened to God.

God told Noah

to build an ark.

And Noah did.
He made it big
and strong
and long
and wide.

He made a window
at the top.
He made a door
in the side.

God told Noah
to put food
in the ark.
And Noah did.

He put in hay
and seeds
and fruits
and vegetables.

God told Noah
to take animals
into the ark.
And Noah did.

He took in two
of every kind.

He took in frogs

and lizards

and birds

and beetles.

He took in camels

and bears

and lions

and monkeys.

In they went,
through the door.

In they went,
two by two.

God told Noah
to bring in
his family.
And Noah did.

He brought in

his wife

and his sons

and his sons' wives

and his grandchildren.

God said:

"I will send
a great flood.
It will rid
the world
of wickedness."

Noah watched
the rain begin
to fall.

The rain fell for forty day

and nights.

The water
covered
everything.

Noah's ark
floated
on the water.

Everyone

inside the ark

was saved.

Then God
sent a wind.
The wind
dried up
the water.

The ark
came to rest.

Noah sent out
a dove.

The dove
came back
with a twig.

Everyone wanted
to go outside.
But Noah waited.

Then one day
Noah opened
the door.

The sun was shining.
Out came the animals,
two by two.

Noah looked up.

He saw a great

rainbow

in the sky.

Then God said:
"I will never
send a great flood
again."

God told Noah
to make a new world.
And Noah did.